SILENT PRESENCE

Discernment as Process and Problem

by

ERNEST E. LARKIN, O. Carm.

DIMENSION BOOKS INC.
DENVILLE, NEW JERSEY 07834

Published by Dimension Books, Inc.

PO Box 811
Denville New Jersey 07834

ISBN: 0-87193-172-9

TABLE OF CONTENTS

PART ONE

THE PROBLEM OF DISCERNMENT

Until recently discernment has not been a high priority among Catholics. We have lived off rules of thumb in doctrine and practice, preferring assembly line religion to a personal and custom-made response to God from deep within our own lives. We have seldom connected our lives with the New Testament teaching that Christianity is a Person, Jesus Christ, and that he lives on in us through the Spirit, who leads us back to the Father. We have neglected the personal action of the Spirit in our life, the mystery of the two freedoms, God's and our own, touching and interacting with one another.

There are historical reasons for this. They go back as far as the inevitable institutionalizing of religion, like the Constantinian shift to Christendom in the fourth century, and they are as modern as the wholesale rejection of the mystical tradition in the 18th and 19th centuries. The New Testament and Patristic teaching on the role of the Spirit are being restored now, and one instance of that effort is the recovery of the tradition on discernment.

Contemplation and personal discernment are

recognized today as normal developments in the spiritual life. Both are experiences of the indwelling God; they are gifts that represent considerable growth and expertise in the life of the Spirit. Both are articulations of the goals of Christian life.

Contemplation and discernment deal directly with the mysterious, incomprehensible God who appears among us and is experienced in himself (in contemplation) or in a given human situation (in discernment). Discernment asks us to be contemplatives in action, in our human choices, finding the same God outside whom we discover in silent prayer. The challenge of identifying that Presence in such a way as to interpret the course of action we should take is a formidable one. It involves our own opaqueness and almost infinite possibility of self-deception. No wonder we shy away from it and seek refuge in the rote answer.

But settled stable answers are becoming increasingly impossible in our transitional world. The knowledge explosion in religion as well as science, gigantic cultural shifts in the world and church, pluralism, personalism, Freud and Marx and armies of interpreters they have spawned have made discernment both more necessary and more difficult than ever. There are fewer certainties, more questions, and greater difficulty in knowing even where to begin the inquiry. We have been party to a revolution in thinking about the human person and the world with the result that our feelings are being reassessed and our behavior reinterpreted. There are fewer landmarks and fewer signposts along the way as our theology and our psychology scramble to meet this new experience.

We find ourselves in a crisis of trust, a loss of

nerve. Does God really speak to me? Or am I a pawn of the system and an automaton before unconscious determinisms? These are questions for our post-Christian secularized world. Do they bespeak lack of faith? The language and the feeling seem to say yes, but maybe we are only reacting against a too facile "God-talk" that has domesticated God, put him in a box, and erased all problems of identifying his will. We have all met the folks who have a direct telephone line to God and always know what he is saying. Their opposing numbers sometime overreact and become so skeptical, so timid, that only another Sinai would give them a sense of certitude that God is dealing with them in their vocation and ministry. They do not deny God's providence. They just don't know how it works. So they prefer to act as if God adapts himself to their choices, even their mistakes. Thus God tags along rather than leads.

There is a good deal to be said in favor of this theology, but it must not undermine the role of God in the relationship. Discernment needs to be re-thought in this new context.

Emotional hang-ups, unconscious projections (which the Jungian specialist Robert M. Doran, S.J., equates with the "disordered affections" that keep all spirituality infantile), compulsions and obsessions, all are severe blocks to spiritual discernment. These are sophisticated psychological insights into the contemporary person that call into question our ability to know ourselves and make objective decisions. In different terminology they were always one of the obstacles in spiritual discernment. Basically *the* difficulty in all discernment is personal inauthenticity. If you are not in touch with yourself, if you don't know what is going on, you cannot hear the "other," even when the Other is God.

Some of these personal difficulties arise from the social environment in which we live. We do not see the systemic evils and the sinful structures that warp our thinking and willing in unconscious ways and make it difficult to tell good from bad. Most of our blindspots come from our own mysterious selves, which have become even more an enigma since the discovery of the unconscious. Is it possible to create a theology of discernment in the light of these difficulties? I think so. But since these difficulties were always, in one way or another, the obstacles to spiritual discernment, I propose that we begin our study by reviewing the traditional theory that has come down to us from Scripture and the Fathers of the Desert. Seeing this body of teaching in its simplest lines will provide a framework in which to critique the process in the light of present perspectives.

I will present the tradition in the form it comes to us in Ignatius of Loyola. According to Hugo Rahner, Ignatius simply codified the tradition developed in Cassian and the Desert Fathers. His brother Karl Rahner in his famous essay entitled, "The Logic of Concrete Individual Knowledge in Ignatius Loyola,"[1] makes the claim that Ignatius offers "the first and till now the only detailed attempt" to identify the process of discovering the will of God. This present essay does not purport to be a full discussion of discernment in its peculiar Ignatian characteristics. Rather it is a presentation of the general theory of the Church's tradition under the guidance of St. Ignatius. His teaching has become common Church patrimony. I assume the responsibility for the positions taken and blame neither Ignatius nor his interpreters for them, though I trust I am not misrepresenting him.

ONE

WHAT IS DISCERNMENT?

Discernment is not one discrete act in the spiritual life, but rather the whole spiritual endeavor. It is like contemplation, which is more an abiding condition of knowing God than a single act. Sometimes contemplation is defined in deceptively simple terms as "a gaze." It is more than that. Contemplation is the knowledge a friend has of a friend; it is deeply personal, experiential, the knowledge that comes from love. It is not bound to any particular form or expression, such as prayer in quietude, but it happens as well in the hurly-burly of a family or in the majestic celebration of Midnight Mass. In a similar fashion discernment should not be regarded as a litmus test, to be applied at key moments of decision. It is spirituality in the concrete, because spirituality is precisely the Spirit *acting* within us and discernment is the awareness of that action.

Spirituality has long suffered from being identified as a theory to be applied; it is life first and only then reflection on life. It is *experiencing* with understanding and commitment the presence and guidance of God in one's whole life. That is discernment too.

Discernment is thus a life work. Paul writes: "Do not be conformed to this world but be transformed by the renewal of your mind, that you may experience what is the will of God, what is good and acceptable and perfect." (Rm. 12:2) Discernment is "experiencing what is the will of God" and it is the consequence of transformation in Christ. Discernment accompanies growth in the love of God (Phil. 1:9-10) and it is the touchstone, the test of the faith. (2 Cor. 13:5)

Only the Spirit can work the transformation, this re-birth or adoption into divine sonship or daughter-hood. "For those who are led by the Spirit of God are the sons of God." (Rm. 8:14) But not every move-ment, even in the children of God, comes from the Holy Spirit. St. John says categorically: "Beloved, do not believe every spirit, but test the spirits to see whether they are of God." (1 John 4:1) A solid personal spirituality is the only consistent ground for distinguishing good and bad impulses, tendencies, aspirations, and decisions. Anything less is magical. Thus the Desert Fathers always identified *discretio* ("discretion" or "discernment") as the achievement of full Christian maturity.

It may be a help to list some modern definitions of discernment. Note that none of these definitions emphasize solving a problem or finding an answer. They underline the fact that discernment is awareness of inner states and the ability to so interpret these states that one's life can be gently guided by the Spirit of God. The goal is tuning into the Spirit; the process is to sift the affective movements within consciousness which have come to be designated as good and bad "spirits."[2]

One author calls discernment "the very dynamic of a faith open to the Spirit and not dependent on

rules and regulations that bind to a static past."[3]
Edward Malatesta identifies discernment of spirits as
"the process by which we examine, in the light of faith
and in the connaturality of love, the nature of the
spiritual states we experience in ourselves and in
others."[4] George Aschenbrenner puts the matter
clearly in a recent *Review for Religious:* "Discernment of spirits involves chiefly an interpretive sorting
out in faith of inner, affective experiences, so that,
through dealing properly with the experiences, one
can find and be with God in every situation and
moment of life."[5]

What is it like to walk with Spirit?

TWO

WAYS TO DISCERN

St. Ignatius has two sets of directives for discernment of spirits, which are tied into the four week program of the *Spiritual Exercises,* his manual for directors of the long retreat. He calls them rules for the First Week and the Second Week respectively, terms which will be explained momentarily. I should like to add a third approach to the work of discerning. Unlike Ignatius' ways, which endeavor to deal directly with the affectivity and utilize the insights gained to locate the action of God in the soul, this third way is more intellectual and abstract. It is the application of a theory of spirituality to one's life. This project, unlike the two "Weeks," especially the Second Week, will not reveal God's particular will. But it does give a necessary understanding and hence direction to a life. We shall begin with it.

First Way: *Application of Spiritual Doctrine*

As Christians we belong to a community that is heir to a well-developed spirituality and doctrine of discernment. Sacred Scripture is the primary hermeneutic interpreting our personal experience, but the *empty vessel medit.—Jack*

whole tradition of the Church, manifested especially in the writings of the Fathers and spiritual masters, helps us understand what is true and false spiritual growth. Generally these documents present particular syntheses of Christian living: Teresa of Avila and John of the Cross, for example, constellating everything around the way of prayer, Ignatius finding the unifying principle in service and abnegation, Cassian in humility, and so forth. All of these masters help us interpret what is going on in our journey to the Father.

Teilhard de Chardin, a modern master, lays down two gospel imperatives, self-development and renunciation. The first call of the gospel, he says, is to utilize our talents, develop our gifts, and construct our human life. Only then does the call to total abnegation make sense. We are called to renounce everything and give our life totally back to God. But we must first possess that life in order to give it away. This double principle is sometimes forgotten, as if the only law were the cross. John of the Cross, for example, dispenses with a long exposition of the first element, since he is not writing for "beginners." But he gives clear indications that he is presupposing this first stage of the process and addresses persons who are ready for the next step, which is contemplation.

The first step, on the other hand, is the aspect of spirituality most discussed in our time in popular spiritual literature. In view of the total gospel, however, this aspect is more like the psychological underpinnings or pre-spirituality. When some contemporary literature treats development as if it were the totality of the effort, we are in danger of neglecting one half of our tradition. It is calamitous to limit the following of Christ to an either/or approach in these two elements or to fail to correlate the positive, developmental, incarnational emphasis with first steps and the self-denying, transcendent, eschatological aspect with the maturing of the faith. Actually a full-blown incarnationism implicitly contains total abnegation, as indeed does a healthy supernaturalism completely honor the legitimate demands of human development. But each concept unpacks different aspects of the one mystery and helps to assure the proper balance of both aspects at appropriate stages of growth.

The formulation of authentic spirituality can never be a single issue spirituality, reducing the whole thrust to prayer, or ministry, or personal integration alone. Spirituality is all these things. It consists in three basic relationships: to self, to God, and to others. These are like three angles of a triangle and the spiritual life is the circular movement that transcribes these three angles. The relationship to self is primarily the recognition of brokenness, to God the attitude of trust, and to others dialogue. All three qualities are constitutive of Christian spirituality. They are as old as the New Testament and as contemporary as Alcoholics Anonymous. The dynamic is the recognition of one's own neediness, a fact that is possible only in the presence of the love of God. God's unconditional love is mediated to us in prayer and community. God loves us first (Rm. 5:5) and this makes self-acceptance possible. At the same time community or dialogue is the normal environment for relationship with God.

Unless one has an understanding of these three pillars of spiritual development, "discernment" becomes an expression of cultural conditioning that mirrors the erstwhile values of the group. One need only read the recent article by Henri Nouwen entitled, "The Monk and the Cripple: Toward a Spirituality of Ministry," to see how foundational these three points are. Nouwen develops the traditional Christian basis of ministry in terms as rigorous as anything John of the Cross has written. The article is a good test case for where our theology of ministry stands, or for that matter, what we think to be the nature of Christian spirituality itself. My guess is that some would find his approach negative, repressive, and pessimistic. But in fact he is presenting a beautiful summary of the pure fonts of our tradition. His article is a help to discernment in ministry. It will not perhaps solve any particular problems in ministerial choices, but it will give direction and guidance in our thinking. While this teaching which is found in all the masters will not tell us where God is at in ministry, it certainly will give us clues as to where we might look and where we need not bother to look. Spiritual theology is thus a remote and general means for spiritual discernment.

Second Way: Recognizing Feelings

The second method of discernment, proper to the First Week of the *Spiritual Exercises,* attempts to utilize affective resonances to find one's way, not as direct indicators of God's particular will, but as experiences to be reckoned with at the beginning of the journey. The affective movements in question are feelings of attraction or repulsion, pulls toward or away from God which Ignatius calls consolations and desolations respectively. These feelings, moods, sentiments, affections are movements of the good or bad spirits within a person and are rooted, therefore, in the Holy Spirit or his counterpart, Satan. The Christian wayfarer is urged to recognize and interpret the predictible movements of these spirits in order to capitalize on the good psychological-spiritual states and avoid injury from the bad ones.

The theology of the *Exercises* is not dependent on Ignatius' medieval world-view of angels and devils. His use of the two spirits struggling for dominance in the soul is the imagery of the times. But the meaning is the biblical struggle between the Spirit and the flesh, between grace and sin, between Christ and Satan, the inevitable war between the forces of good and evil. Ignatius' angelology and demonology are beside the point. Nor is a particular theology of providence essential for following Ignatius' rules, such as the non-Ignatian caricature of an excessively vertical and hierarchical God who makes all the decisions antecedently without any involvement of our freedom and gives to us only the task of dis- covering that master plan. God does not make choices for us but with us in the relationship of infinite love. Neither is the perspective of the *Exercises* a Jesus- and-me piety, though like Counter-reformation spirituality in general, Ignatius betrays a heavy emphasis on the individual relationship with God. We are interested in the riches of his insights into the process of Christian growth, which are perennial and beyond the limitation of his own religious culture.

The First Week's discernment, for "beginners," applies to those who are working through their first conversion. Persons of the First Week have a funda- mental orientation to God but they lack "indiffer- ence." Indifference is an Ignatian term that is equi- valent to John of the Cross' "detachment," and intelligible to most people today as "biblical faith." It is a complete openness to God, a freedom, the ability to move in whatever direction God calls. People in the First Week lack this developed love of God. They are still hung up on their own pleasure and pain, their own gratification, and self-will. By definition the Second Week comprises those who have this indifference, either as a temporary state of fervor induced by the retreat or as an achieved growth in the Spirit that characterizes their lives. Ignatius' directives are set down in two series of "rules," called "Rules for perceiving and understanding to some degree the different movements that are produced in the soul." Note he does not use the verb *discerner* (discerning) but *sentir* (feeling) and *cognoscer* (experiencing). Ignatius will help the retreatant discern, not by applying general principles to individual cases, but by helping him perceive and evaluate the movements in his heart. This is the key to all real discernment.

The "feeling" or "experiencing" of the movements in the First Week puts one on guard but does not give a positive direction to take. Reason or reflection does that, for the norm of judging here is prudence, that is "right reason for acting" *(recta ratio agibilium)*. Reason, not feelings as such, is to guide the person who is trying to consolidate his life in the Lord.

How is the Spirit guiding this process of conversion? By calling the retreatant to repent and to hold the line against all contrary feelings. The Spirit is actively involved in the positive movements, as is the evil spirit in the contrary movements. Ignatius calls the retreatant to "perceive and understand" these movements for what they are, not in order to know God's individual will, which at this time is clear enough, but as encouragements and warnings, helps and hindrances to be faithful to the struggle going on in a divided, ambivalent, but good-willed Christian.

The person is not free enough at this time to interpret the resonances of God's action in his soul in any more directive way. The task is purification that leads to freedom. When that freedom has been won, a more direct communication can take place between the divine and human freedoms in this love affair, and the "regulation" of this interchange is addressed in the Second Week.

The movements or feelings at this point are thus to be treated as children in a bygone era — they are to be seen and not heard. Ignatius, familiar as he is with the ways of God, helps the beginner to see what is going on, what generally takes place in conversion and how one best deals with the subtle feelings that pull him to and fro. At this point, therefore, they have only relative value. The beginning Christian is too filled with himself, too hung up with his own neurotic needs, his lack of self-knowledge and self-discipline, his infantile motivations of self-gratification to allow feelings to chart the course. Instead he is to follow the wisdom of his tradition and rise above feelings, not serving God and neighbor when he "feels" like it and neglecting duty when the attraction has passed. Rather he is to settle on a good program of spiritual growth and set his face toward Jerusalem.

This is the period in which he is formed by the community tradition. In this task he is listening to God's spokesmen and delegates rather than directly to the Lord himself. The feelings sometimes reinforce the new way of life chosen and then they are "consolidations" or they will pull in the opposite direction and then they are "desolations." Consolations for Ignatius are whatever help you to love God more. They have little or nothing to do with euphoria. Desolation is an affective pull away from God. The anguished sense of loss of a loved one may be a consolation, because it draws one closer to God, whereas the euphoric feeling of a person who is imbibing too much alcohol is desolation.

In the First Week, then, neither consolations or desolations are to be interpreted as a definitive word from the Lord, a prophetic message. So the words of the song, "It can't be wrong when it feels so right," are a poor norm for a person at this stage of development. It may be that it feels so "right," because the feeling comes from the flesh.   *?*

All this must sound familiar to anyone brought up in the pre-Vatican II Church. Spiritual formation in novitiates, seminaries, and parish churches had one rule about the affectivity: "Pay no attention to feelings. Keep the rule and the rule will keep you." This was acceptable, to a point, for beginners. What is not intelligible is that this kind of formation was the whole project with no further objective proposed. It was education for mediocrity.

Third Way: Interpreting Feelings

The direction Ignatius gives for the Second Week is predicated on the conviction that God does speak to us personally in the ordinary course of his providence and that we can hear him through our affective experiences. Sacred Scripture is filled with the affirmation. God's language, however, is not words or sound waves but "the effect he produces in our souls."[8] This implies the "spiritual illumination" which Aquinas defined as "a certain inner and intelligible light which elevates the mind so that it can perceive things that understanding cannot perceive through its natural light."[9] But the illumination is the interpretation, not the communication of God's word as such. In Ignatian discernment the affectivity bears the message and through the reading of our interior experience we receive a "prophetic word from God,"[10] addressed to us individually and concretely, an invitation to a certain course of action, to a vocation, a project, a way of serving in the world today. The experience of that word from God, of that effect experienced in one's being, is the experience of discernment. It is hearing and responding to the word of God by one who knows the language. The Second Week offers help in learning and interpreting that language and responding appropriately.

The affectivity is interpreted by the fruit it produces, but this fruit is not precisely or at least entirely the action undertaken. Bad actions are indeed one indication, namely, they are a proof of God's absence. But good actions are not necessarily proof of his presence. Jesus said: "A good tree cannot bear bad fruit any more than a bad tree can bear good fruit . . . You can tell a tree by its fruits." (Matt. 7:18, 20) What is the fruit in question? Paul gave the answer in Galatians 5:16-25, the *locus classicus* for the criteria of Christian discernment. It is very important to interpret this passage carefully, lest we be misled into simply identifying fruits and actions.

THREE

BAD FRUIT

Bad fruits are bad works; the feelings do not count here. "But I say," says St. Paul, "walk by the Spirit, and do not gratify the desires of the flesh. Now *the works* of the flesh are plain: immorality, impurity, licentiousness, idolatry, sorcery, enmity, strife, jealousy, anger, selfishness, dissension, party spirit, envy, drunkenness, carousing, and the like." (Gal. 5:16, 19-21 RSV translation, italics added.) The criteria are works (ta erga). Here is the first rule for all discernment: sinful behavior is contradictory to God's will. Bad works are like a neon sign lighting up the fact that God is not present in the action.

Whatever the matter in question, however speciously justifiable or apparently logical, whether the reason for the course of action comes from a long process of inquiry or is a supposed direct "inspiration" of God, if the project is accompanied by or productive of immoral behavior or uncharitable acts it is certain that the action in question is not of God. What may seem to have begun in God has ended in the flesh, and the devil has once again transformed himself into an angel of light (2 Cor. 11:14). This principle applies both to the individual and the community.

Famous examples in the lives of the saints abound, like the story attributed to St. Philip Neri, who was asked to render a judgment on a would-be ecstatic of the time. His first question to her was this: "Is it not surprising that the Lord would choose you for this special grace?" When the nun became angry and protested vigorously how deserving she was of God's special favor, the interview was terminated by St. Philip. The obvious pride had given the lie to any claims of a special grace in Philip's mind.

Another example is Paul's complaint to a divided Corinthian church that he could not speak to them "as spiritual men and women, but as persons of the flesh," ready only for milk and not solid food. "For while there is jealousy and strife among you, are you not of the flesh, and behaving like ordinary men and women?" (1 Cor. 3:1-3) The divisions, the destructive cliques, the pride and vanity were signs that the influence of the Spirit was absent.

This is a practical rule for our own choices. If in seeking out or exercising a ministry, you must stoop to immoral means or you cause hatred and dissension to prevail; if you must manipulate, use deceit, and lord it over others to get your way; if you do not do the loving thing, which is not always the sweet thing and sometimes is the tough thing, yet done in love; your performance in that ministry is not of the Spirit. *The Woman of the Pharisees* of Francois Mauriac illustrates this principle in the subtle spiritual pride and misguided zeal of the protagonist that almost destroyed a parish. The bad fruit was the destroying of reputations, dividing marriage partners, and undermining the pastor's authority. Yet all the while the woman's intentions were good. The evil spirit was at work.

You may say that this principle negates the mission of the unpopular prophet who speaks hard truths to the community. Inevitably he causes divisions and hostilities. The difference here is that the authentic prophet does not cause but simply surfaces sinful situations already there, whether they are personal or systemic, and he does so for the good of the community. He opens the wound in order to heal, and this is a witness of fraternal love. Ultimately, greater love hopefully will prevail in the community, but even this is not certain. The prophet may be rejected and the sinful conditions continue. But in any case he is not guilty of sin nor are his actions wrong. The community or the individuals are being challenged to rise out of their sin.

FOUR

GOOD FRUIT

The fruit of the Holy Spirit is not works as such, but spirituality, that is, inner life and power. "The fruit of the Spirit is love, joy, peace, patience, kindness, goodness, faithfulness, gentleness, self-control." (Gal. 5:22) These good fruits are attitudes of mind and heart; they are of course incarnated in good actions, but the fruit is not just the particular action. Good actions can be counterfeited and be phony. The Spirit's presence is evident therefore only in the "experiential experience," to use Mouroux's term, the deep existential reality in the situation, and not just in the empirical, externally verifiable reality. Ignatian consolation is the love, peace, joy and all the other marvelous gifts of the indwelling Spirit. Good works as works are always equivocal. They prove nothing. Only authentic spiritual experience cannot be counterfeited and this is the criterion Paul lays down for the presence of the Spirit.

The rules for discernment in the Second Week are based on the fact that good people are not tempted by obvious evil, but only by evil under the appearance of good. The mature Christian is one deeply rooted in God; he or she is not lightly disturbed by the appeals of the senses and worldly attractions. Good people by definition are wedded to the good, but they are tempted by apparent goods that are camouflaged evils. From Cassian to Merton this has been the constant warning of spiritual masters to the pious: your pious sentimentality will betray you; your unrealistic idealism will trip you up. To the zealous, they say: beware of your aggressiveness, your righteousness; it will easily become hardness and lack of compassion. The contemplatives are warned about multiplying fasts and vigils that weaken their health and, therefore, their ability to pray at all. Or else they are called to task for laziness, the occupational hazard of their state of life.

Good people get in trouble because they are taken unawares by evils that look like goods. The workaholic things that he or she is being super zealous for the kingdom of God, all the while neglecting "the one thing necessary." The professional "nice guy" or "sweet gal" is always soft and gentle because they cannot bring themselves to own their own anger and in this way they refuse to bring a part of themselves into the light to be healed by the Lord. Good actions prove nothing; it is the Spirit that counts. That is why the criterion of the Second Week is not what is morally justifiable, but what is spiritually productive. The criterion is faith, hope and charity.

The affectivity thus bears the whole weight of discernment in the second stage, as reason did in the First Week. The positive feelings here are not just human emotions, but movements of the spiritual affectivity which may or may not overflow into the body or psyche and manifest themselves as obvious human emotions. We need not be clinical here. We are dealing with the human being and all the levels of his or her feelings, but directly we are concerned with the spiritual feelings which are sometimes very "unemotional." The feelings in question are like real knowledge as opposed to notional knowledge, evaluative cognition compared with abstract information.

The pleasure-pain dyad has little in common with consolation and desolation; it is often a poor index even of joy and sorrow. The fruits of the Spirit in St. Paul's descriptive catalogue are manifestations of deep spirituality, and spirituality as such thrives in dryness as well as sweetness, in the dark night of St. John of the Cross as well as the delight *(gustos)* of St. Teresa of Avila. We can also spare ourselves the trouble of trying to distinguish between what is of grace and what is of nature in these feelings. This is an impossible task, because concretely the double element works together in graced person. Sometimes people ask, "Is it my idea or is it God speaking to me?" It is likely both (if it is spiritually productive), because God ordinarily works through secondary causes. The inquisitors asked Joan of Arc if her "voices" were from God. When she replied yes, they said, "Come now, they are from your imagination." "Of course," Joan replied, "how else could God speak to us?"

The theologian needs to search out the mechanisms, but the spiritual criterion for God's presence is more simple. If the Lord is present and acting, the signs will be there: a joy even in suffering, for example, or peace even in persecution. On the other hand the joy may explode in great euphoria and the peace manifest itself in demonstrable equanimity. The distinctions here are sometimes so subtle that only the person who has experienced them can tell the difference. This is why the first quality of the spiritual director, who helps discern the action of the Spirit, is his own personal experience. Discernment is not learned from books.

FIVE

DISCERNMENT IN HUMAN TERMS

The processes described are not artificial or superimposed; they are organic to the person's life. A distinct issue can be prayed over, studied and interpreted. But discernment can never be successfully carried out if it is only an occasional act that is foreign to one's usual total life. We discern as well as we live, and we live as well as we discern. Dom Chapman made the same observation about prayer.

Today in our anthropocentric culture in which theology has become anthropology, the fruits of the Spirit need to be translated into the human quality of the Christian life. Only then will they be seen as realities that track the way of God in our personal life or in the human community. To attempt to see these Christian perfections in their human dress, shining through the inevitable ambiguities and paradoxes of existence, is to see how discernment ideally is always taking place.

The person in tune with the Spirit is a free and loving human being, who no longer depends on self-gratification or self-aggrandizement for happiness. His or her strength comes from deep within where the Spirit dwells. They are persons of peace and joy, because they have what they want; openness to truth and goodness, union with the Father of lights from whom every best gift descends. These persons can be in disturbing circumstances, having just lost a job or even a loved one, yet there is a basic peace in their hearts in spite of the grief. They are on top of their life. Emotions come and go and they are sensitive enough to recognize and own all of them. But they do not control. These people are free, that is to say "indifferent" or "detached." This means that they are their own persons in Jesus Christ, committed yet full of strong feelings that run the gamut of human emotions. This human quality stands out in the way they relate to brothers and sisters, to ministry, to the world both in its grandeur and tragedy.

Above all they carry their brothers and sisters in their hearts and identify with their suffering even when their own circumstances spare them from material want or political oppression. Yet this does not relieve them of sadness, worry or anger over adverse conditions in others. They deal with these things as real concern and love others whether there is any return or not, even when rebuffed or not accepted. In ministry they move where the Spirit leads them, perhaps into militancy, perhaps studies, perhaps to the humble service of the poor. But their life shows them becoming more and more human, more deeply joyful, more loving.

These qualities, all of them fruits of the Spirit, become less and less an occasional experience and more and more a permanent condition as they grow in holiness. The fruits define the saints of God, so that it is no surprise that these people respond to what is good and true connaturally, congruently, by second nature. They resonate with what is of God, because they are of God. Whatever is contrary to that ideal rubs the wrong way and causes distress, anxiety, and desolation.

How do we achieve this blessed state? By growth in discernment, which, it should be clear, is God's work in us, the salvation promised us in Jesus Christ. But there are ways to collaborate under grace in this growth. This is the "how to" question, which will occupy the second part of this book.

PART II

THE PROCESS OF PERSONAL DISCERNMENT

We have seen that discernment identifies the Spirit of God at work in an individual or a community in three different ways. We come to recognize that Presence by seeing the lines of authentic gospel spirituality emerging and possessing the person. This first way is an intellectualist kind of discernment, ① limited in its usefulness. We move closer to identifying God's particular will when we examine the "movements" going on in the person or community. The movements are resonances in the sensible or spiritual affectivity rooted in sin or grace, the evil spirit or the Holy Spirit. A second mode of discern- ② ment is to recognize these movements as signs of the struggle going on between good and evil within oneself and use these manifestations of consolation and desolation as insights and energies to help us on our way; this is Ignatius' counsels for the First Week. ③ Or we can read the signs as God's very language, eg I Ching indicating in the projects and decisions associated with the positive affective experience a word from the Lord interpreting the given event in our life. In this third way we tune into what is God's word for us at the particular moment.

This is the basic framework of discernment in the *Spiritual Exercises.* Discernment moves ever deeper within, seeking contact with the indwelling Spirit. It is growth in contemplation. Discernment adds to contemplation the human event. John of the Cross was satisfied to lead the soul into divine union, to help the person dwell in the center of his/or her life where he/she could be touched by divine love. He has relatively little doctrine on discernment; it is sufficient for him to get beyond limited human ways of perceiving and judging and move to the level of spirit in pure faith, there to be embraced by divine love. His is a nuptial or spousal spirituality. Ignatius, however, has the same high mystical union in view, but it is found above all in apostolic action. Discernment is key to his thinking, because his goal is union with the "working God" *(Deus operarius)* with whom he collaborates in building up the Kingdom.

THREE EXPERIENCES OF DIVINE LOVE

All union with God comes from "the love of God poured forth in our hearts by the Holy Spirit who is given to us." (Rm. 5:5) This love is received according to the manner and measure of the receiver. In the beginning the person is divided in heart, ambivalent about God, distracted and pulled by many desires. At this stage God's love struggles with selfishness for dominance, and one learns how to recognize and take advantage of the pulls toward God (consolations) and the pulls away from him (desolations) to consolidate and deepen the contact with God. Once one moves into the center of one's life, in the illuminative way (Second Week), the love of God that has been struggling against the powers of darkness is experienced more immediately and empirically, either in an unbrooked outpouring of love that brings a total surrender of the person, or in historical incarnations of that love that are partial, fragmentary, and intermittent.

Karl Rahner identifies the first of these two experiences of divine love as "consolation without previous cause;" it is the experience of pure transcendence. The second movements of consolation are disparate impulses of the affectivity that are tied into particular events, ideas, or decisions. They are limited, categorical expressions of the unlimited divine love; they alternate with the absence of consolation, without and with previous cause, are like the charismatic and the christic expressions of Christian life, pure grace or grace concretized in a human container, the transcendent or the incarnational manifestations of God. Examples of the experience of pure transcendence are moments of contemplation, such as the spiritual delight (gustos) which Teresa of Avila equates with the prayer of quiet. Perhaps an even better example is the profound identification with God that is the mystical union and causes ineffable knowledge, joy and peace, and sometimes brings with it "a spirit of prophecy and the grace St. Paul terms the discernment of spirits," according to St. John of the Cross.[11] Such mystical moments are by no means restricted to the extraordinary or the higher realms of mystical life. They are empirical experiences of falling in love that is the state of grace given to all who are in the Spirit and this experience can happen to any Christian.[12] Categorical consolations-desolations are the peace, love, constancy, joy and the opposite numbers associated with particular events in the give and take of life's daily experiences. Both ways of God's touching provide an entré to God's particular will by giving the sign of approval to decisions associated with the consolation.

Ignatius speaks of a third way (the third mode of election), which is more cerebral, consisting as it does in a more rational lining up of pros and cons for a particular decision. This last and least form of discernment technique was wrongly held till recently to

be the normal way of making a particular decision.
Today it is generally agreed that for Ignatius the
second way is the usual one; the third way is chosen
only when the "spirits" are not moving in the person's
soul and even then the third way seeks confirmation
of the decision by praying for the movements of
consolation-desolation. Feelings, affections, Pascal's
"heart" are the royal road to Christian discernment,
always of course through interpreting their meaning
in a wise fashion.

The consolation without previous cause is the *Iething grace*
root of all discernment through the affective movements. When that love breaks into our lives, we are at
that moment caught up and totally open to God.
There is no longer both yes and no in our response, no
consolation-desolation, but pure consolation, hence
pure yes to God. It is the way of Jesus before the
Father and Paul claims it for himself. (2 Cor. 1:18-19)
The experience is one of profound Christ-centered-
ness; for as long as it lasts, the person is totally in the
Father's will. The experience also provides the capa-
bility of a "discerning heart" for subsequent concrete
events. Later understandings and decisions can be
recognized as particular, concrete, categorical expressions of this same love. They are reflections, off-
shoots, participations like a lighted wick from a
blazing fire. Or else those ideas and projects are
shown up in the light of that divine love to be
counterfeits, aliens, and enemies. Without the original
experience of pure love discernment could not take
place. The centering in Christ is the first principle in
the order of action, like the principle of contradiction
in the order of knowledge.

Actions, attitudes, decisions which express in a
partial way the love of God which in itself is unlimited

will resonate favorably and produce joy, peace, love. They will be like a drop of water on a sponge. The loving person and the loving action are concordant; they "fit;" they "make music" together. The opposite is also true. Actions that are not in God, that are not loving, that are false or evil in their origin and orientation will clash with the deepest self, like a drop of water hitting rock. There will be discord, lack of resonance, conflict, dividedness. The process is a practical syllogism with the end in view (an unlimited love of God) acting as the major, the problem in question (a choice to be made) simulating the minor, and the conclusion emerging as consonance or dissonance, peace or discord. The judgment is fashioned in one's center or heart, not on the level of mere human emotion. The latter is the announcement of what has taken place within. For this reason only the centered person, centered temporarily or habitually, can discern spirits by this method of Ignatius. He/she is the "spiritual person" St. Paul describes in the first three chapters of 1 Corinthians. "The natural man does not accept what is taught by the Spirit of God. For him, that is absurdity. He cannot come to know such teaching because it must be apprised in a spiritual way. The spiritual man, on the other hand, can appraise everything, though he himself can be appraised by no one." (1 Cor. 2:14-15)

TWO

DEVELOPING DISCERNMENT SKILLS

What is second nature to the spiritual person is practiced and developed by those journeying forward. This is done by exercises in discernment. The danger is that we come to think of such endeavors simplistically, as easy techniques to be had for the asking. People will say: "Pray over the matter, and God will let you know." This is an over-simplication. Discernment is not a mechanical procedure.

I would like to quote a paragraph from a brochure published for private use describing the consciousness-examen, an exercise in Ignatian discernment based on matching particular experiences with the experience of being surrendered or centered. The quotation reads:

> This experience [of being centered in God] now becomes the touchstone of my life — the experience against which I test all my other experiences to see if they square with that feeling of being "at home" with God.
>
> If I take each present interior experience and drop it down inside myself at that level where I am still trying to live out my total surrender, my "Yes, Father," and if it fits into that stance before God, then this will be a sign to me that it is right and good and from God. There will be a sense of rightness, peace and joy.[13]

The description is only a part of a whole article, but even so the paragraph presumes a great deal. It presumes a Christ-centered person with a discerning heart, a person in touch with his fundamental option experientially and skilled in interpreting conscious feelings. For many the description represents a goal to be accomplished rather than a method to be implemented at will. The technique does not operate in computer fashion. It works only when the person dwells deeply in the Spirit and from that stance evaluates the individual experience.

This process, in other words, presumes a great deal of spiritual development. It presumes the whole work of purification, not as a totally accomplished fact, but well enough established and continuing to mature. The rational has gained the upper hand over errant emotions and the whole person become docile, flexible, open to the stirrings of the Spirit within.

This work of the First Week is no mean achievement. It means that a great deal of self-knowledge has been gained. The discerner has come to terms with his unconscious and is not easily fooled by its tricks, by hearing his own voice, for example, and calling it God's voice, by concluding to do just what he wanted to do anyway independently of God and calling that discernment. The wish can be father to the thought or to the decision. Pious rhetoric can be used to cloak one's own unrecognized needs for domination or self-gratification. The mature Christian knows that we experience what we want and/or expect to experience, and that is the case, not only in extraordinary phenomena, but in ordinary spiritual sentiments and aspirations. All of this has been dealt with in the purifying process.

Besides this presupposition (which is recognized by practitioners and teachers of the consciousness-examen) there is the danger of misrepresenting the method as if it were a revelation of God's will through the back door. Interfacing God and ourselves will reveal one thing: mystery, the mystery of God's boundless love for us, his suffering with us, his incredible gift of himself to us. Discernment will not tell us the technical solution to our problem or give us secret knowledge no one else possesses. Discernment will only give us a sense that we are doing the right thing. The language of discernment for Ignatius as for John of the Cross is the language of wisdom rather than science, of intuition and feeling rather than analysis.

In discernment God is not about to supply individual directions like the answers to Old Testament fleeces or private revelations that remove us from the human condition of not knowing. We live and grow in faith as did Jesus in his earthly existence; how can we expect anything different for ourselves? What the Spirit gives us is reassurance, love, peace and joy, so that we know we are on the right track and that the direction we are taking is Christ-like. The method, therefore, cannot be overly objectified. It will not reveal things to us, only the mystery of persons.

Is there, then, no art of discernment, no process we can follow? Is discernment to come to us by osmosis, as part of the spiritual giftedness of growth in holiness? It is certainly true, as Thomas Dubay points out, that the gospels say nothing about process, which actually is only about two percent of the matter of discernment.[14] But the New Testament deals extensively with the conditions for discernment.

I want to maintain in the rest of this book that these very conditions make discernment possible and can be the principle of a process we may follow. I am convinced that this is not a replacement but a revitalization of the tradition on the process of Christian discernment.

THREE

RENEWAL OF THE DISCERNMENT PROCESS

Theology from above

T. from below

The two models of theology illustrated in contemporary christology, theology from above and from below, might be helpful here. In discernment we need to proceed, not by deducing conclusions from a priori principles from on high as theology from above directs, but rather by becoming empirical, by beginning with feelings, moods, aspirations, trying to understand and evaluate them and thereby enter more deeply into our true selves. This self-knowledge leads to self-acceptance, to owning our true selves, good and bad. A third step is integration, which is a sense of wholeness, of seeing the parts contextualized in the totality and achieving what earlier authors called detachment. Detachment and integration are thus different concepts, but they are descriptive of the same one reality, namely, that of a person in love with God. Detachment and integration are other faces of love. Integration orders our whole life to God. It is a way of measuring our love of God from the viewpoint of the self, just as we can make the same evaluation from the viewpoint of fraternal charity or the love of God in himself. A fourth and final step which

inductive approach

1. Self Knowledge

2. Self acceptance

3. Integrate

4. Validate

accompanies the whole process and confirms the conclusion is validation. Validation refers to the interactional element in discernment and the confirmation by the community of one's interior way.

I submit that these four steps represent a practical and effective way of searching out the direction of God in our lives. They will serve to move us out of a demoralizing outer-directedness into a life-giving inner-directedness that is the leading of the Holy Spirit from within. It is discernment from below, and I suspect that it is the way Ignatius himself proceeded, who always began with what is and then went to the past and future for understanding and decision. I would like now to describe the process in some detail. The four steps — self-knowledge, self-acceptance, integration, and validation — are individual and distinct, but they are interconnected and overlapping. They are not a one-two-three-four step recipe.

Self-knowledge

This is age-old wisdom, the rock-bottom foundation for every spiritual life. Teresa of Avila sees it as part of every dwelling place or mansion in the interior castle, though it belongs especially to the first. What is it? It is to experience yourself, to be in touch with your thinking, your feeling and your behavior, all three together. You "intellectualize" if you identify your experience only with what you think; Decartes' dictum, "I think, therefore I am," is as deficient psychologically as it is philosophically. I am more than my thinking. I am a feeling, imaging, deciding, acting human being.

Feelings likewise are only part of me, but an extremely important part, because they are the real me, the spontaneous me without camouflage and facile misrepresentation. They have, however, been so neglected especially by the last generations of religious people that the individual may not be in touch with them and need the help of a psychological counselor to appropriate them. They remain the most honest reflection of the real me. In themselves they are morally neutral, a precious revelation of what I am really like.

But there is a third element and that is behavior. Thoughts and feelings produce action, and actions speak louder than words or thoughts or feelings. But in themselves they too are ambivalent, or better equivocal. They are never sure-fire indicators of what is deep within. Like all things human, they come forth as a mixture of truth and falsehood, good and bad, beauty and ugliness. So alone and by themselves they are a limited criterion. A knowledge of my real self is the product of all three indications, knowing what I feel, feeling what I know, and acting in the light of both.

The three-pronged approach to authenticity is more difficult to achieve than it seems. From the beginning we hide the truth from ourselves, build defenses against reality, create a false self, which Merton calls the empirical self. Reality threatens, so our defenses create a refuge. We repress our feelings, explain away our narcissism and escape into all kinds of frenetic activity, even and maybe especially into altruistic activity: altruism is one of our defenses. We prefer to dwell in our beseiged little fortress that shuts out reality, or in view of the Marxist social analysis, we settle for being slaves to a system rather than struggling for our own and our brother's birthright of freedom.

What is our worst threat? Ernest Becker says it

is the fear of death, the fear of our own limitations and the limits of life. Sebastian Moore in a recent article on "Christian Self-Discovery" says it is love.[15] Love scares us, because it will not allow us to live in our private, alienated, me-for-me solitude. God's love is a searing power that burns away the layers of falsehood that cover our true selves, viz, being self-transcending lovers.

The layers of falsehood are the reason for the dark night. They are our dark side, our shadow, the evil deep within, and the suffering of the dark night is precisely the experiencing of this negative side of our life. The unconscious becomes conscious and the transposition is a painful one. In the dark nights, says St. John of the Cross, "all of the soul's infirmities are brought to light; they are set before its eyes to be felt and healed."[16] Self-knowledge thus comes at a heavy price, the price of an endless search and an openness that welcomes the painful truth as well as the incredible love of God.

The way of self-knowledge is more contemplative than analytic, more receptive than introspective. You want to learn, so you listen deeply to the divergent feelings, insights, hopes and aspirations. You scan your psyche like a sailor on watch. For spiritual discernment you must be looking and listening from a place deep within, from your center, "the other side of silence." When the listening is that deep, you are facing the relevant questions, whereas the avoidance of these questions is the "basic sin," according to Lonergan.

The fully functioning person, says Carl Rogers, is the one who knows what his or her heart is saying. The heart for the believer is the still point where God and the soul meet. It is the point of contact with God, with the Self which is greater than ourselves, certainly much larger than our ego. In words that resonate with Augustine and are a modern translation of John of the Cross, Thomas Klise writes in *The Last Western:*

> In all true listening the listener opens his spirit to the Loving One, the Power and the Strength as some call Him/Her, the YOU who is wholly Other and yet also wedded to the true self. And it is of the essence in perfection of true listening that once the demands of the normal self have been completely put aside, the voice of the self wedded to Truth and Love speak in such a way to the heart of the listener that he is assured it is no other than the voice of the Loving One Him/Herself and the listener knows this with the exact same degree of certainty that he knows that he exists.[17]

Self-Acceptance

Self-acceptance means to recognize yourself in your thoughts, feelings and behavior. It means to own your good self as well as your bad, your pluses and minuses, exaggerating neither side and being at peace with both. Such acceptance does not mean acting out the evil. Nor does avoiding evil mean crushing it by repression; rather, it means dealing with it, honestly, wisely, courageously. Let your feelings inform you of what is as you stand within the feelings and yet above and beyond them. View them from a deep place within, from your center, because from there you can see them without distortion or enslavement. This journey within takes time, discipline, and experience.

Faith enters the picture, faith and trust in people, in the world, and ultimately in God's unconditioned love and acceptance, mediated by parents, peers, and teachers. I know I am good, because others love me; I can accept my shadow, the evil within, in that context. I can accept myself completely when I am convinced of God's absolute and total love. To cheat, to put blinders on so that I don't see will achieve nothing; I need to face the reality head-on, and when I do that deeply enough, I touch God himself. So it is not only okay to be me, it is pure gift, God loves me as I am; he calls me to repent when I recognize my sin, but in this way the very evil within me becomes part of the beautiful tapestry of my life. God would not allow evil unless he could draw greater good from it, as Augustine said.

Integration

Integration follows from self-knowledge and self-acceptance. Integration is wholeness, each part in its place and all parts seen in the context of the whole. It is healing. It occurs because I know myself, my whole self which reaches all the way into God; I am no longer wearing blinders that control and enslave me. I am "together," ordered, the lower part subservient to the higher and the total related to God. I have that "tranquility of order" which St. Thomas calls peace. It is self-possession, consolation, openness, freedom, detachment, indifference, a trusting spirit, and all the other fruits of the good Spirit. The integration we speak of is the work of grace. For this reason discernment appears at this point.

Once you get to know who you really are in your deepest self, the direction of your life emerges. You are now free enough to sense the movement of God in your life. You know what you mean, what you are about, what is your truth. By the same token you recognize your false self, your shadow that would beguile you into quick success or bogus happiness. To know your truth is to be able to separate what fits you individually from what would destroy you. To know your truth is to know what resonates, what produces peace and joy. Often it has a physical resonance such as a good feeling all over or concentrated in one place like the solar plexus. Such feelings help to identify the evil that lurks under the appearance of good.

Does this way of discernment sound too secular? Where is God in the process? The answer is that he is in the *real*. "The most essential requirement for the development of one's prayer life," writes William Barry, and we can add, for the development of discernment, is "to be as real as one can be before God. The relationship to the Lord is like any other relationship, only more so: it thrives on reality and honesty."[18] In this method we are dealing with the real, our own experience, our own reason and judgment, our language, our world, and once we are deep enough into self-understanding, we simply know what to be "in attunement" to ourselves means and when it does or does not exist. The language is not religious, but the reality is of God. This approach of building from the bottom up instead of using some extrinsic set of rules and applying them from afar involves less danger of deluding ourselves into seeing what we want to see and missing what we want to avoid.

Teresa of Avila and Teilhard de Chardin illustrate the two different movements, from below and from above in two random but complementary statements. Both are saying that once we create space for God, he comes and fills us with himself. Teresa writes: "For it is very certain that in emptying ourselves of all that is creature and detaching ourselves from it for the love of God, the same Lord will fill us with himself."[19] Chardin describes the same experience: "For those in whose eyes God has become the supreme reality in the universe, there can logically be no more stable and profound happiness than to feel this reality painfully taking the place of their own being — insofar as that being has been faithful in shaping and developing itself."[20] Teresa is speaking the language of abstract theology; Chardin's statement is anthropological. Ultimately both are saying the same thing, because God comes to us and relates to us in our human condition. We do not destroy the human in order to become divine. We allow the human to reach its highest potential, to be divinized and possessed by God precisely by undergoing the changes that are God's original will for men and women in their creation. At the deepest level we are "gods;" we are a word of God; this does not take our humanity away but fulfills it. It is this new creation, this new being that hears the word of God resounding in our consciousness and sees it leading us along the labyrinthian ways of our daily experiences that constitutes the spiritual person wholly in tune with God.

Validation

So far I have described the process in individualistic terms. Christian discernment is actually dialogic and interactional in character. The inner principle of life is the object of our search, because this is the indwelling Spirit who gives life; the flesh profits nothing. (John 6:63) But the outer reality is the locus of the human. The flesh redeemed is the way to the Spirit within. God uses the outer aspect of life, which puts us in touch with the world as the vehicle, not only for the final step of discernment which we call validation, but for all the previous steps as well. In this sense discernment is interactional.

Others give me myself, biologically, psychologically, and even spiritually; they give me my faith, the community of the Church, the formation out of which I live. My development on every level is bound up with significant persons, structures, and institutions, and partly because of this fact some of my development is good, some bad. When I take stock and discern what is going on, I need to validate my experience by the same instruments that made me what I am.

Validation comes from my tradition, especially the normative statement of Christian life which is Sacred Scripture, or one of its derivatives, such as the writings of the holy men and women of God from apostolic times to the present. But the living representatives of this tradition — teachers, counselors, spiritual directors — all of whom will help me observe, objectify, and evaluate my experience are also important witnesses. They represent the living community, which is the real *locus* of all discernment; I could not begin to function in the area of discernment without the community. Its contribution is spiritual direction in its myriad forms.

FOUR

PROCESS

The process described is Christian discernment in a modern key. It is psychological, sociological, and anthropological, but its inspiration is spiritual. It has similar stages of growth as the older categories "from above." At an early stage, objective criteria and norms and prudential judgment are the more important guidelines. The person endeavors above all to take possession of his life, to establish himself in a Christian vocation, to choose a project in life. An ego-centered spirituality takes shape and it is good; it is the struggle to respond to God's grace and take one's place in the Christian community. Decisions emerge from the norms of common sense and sound reason, informed psychology and social analysis, all of this enlightened by faith. This state corresponds to the First Week.

But as the person matures there is closer affinity to the well-springs of life, a freer spirit, a more dominant and spontaneous love. This does not mean abstractness. On the contrary, greater particularity is manifest and uniqueness stands out. The uniqueness of each person is the incarnation of the special call of the Holy Spirit that is each one of us. Discernment is by congruence, congeniality, and connaturality. The question is no longer: "Shall I do as the others have done?" It is: "What is the Lord saying to me now?" Now it is a question of a vocation within a vocation, the particulars of my prayer life, my relationships, my ministry, my unique witness in the mystical body of Christ. Union with God and fellow human beings is deep, and union differentiates, as Chardin has emphasized for our time. Each becomes more and more himself/herself in the mystery of Christ.

FIVE

SOME CONCRETE MODELS

There are several popular exercises and practices today that implement the kind of process we have been describing. I shall list a few examples.

1. *Prayer.* Prayer develops the connaturality that is the basis of discernment, namely, an "at-homeness" with one's deepest self and with God. Contemplative prayer, both in forms that employ images, such as Ignatian contemplation, and in image-less, dark contemplation, like centering prayer sensitize oneself to one's deep inner reality. Even the old method of *lectio divina* translated into contemporary terms of listening (reading/meditation), waiting *(oratio* or praying), and experiencing (contemplation) is a paradigm for discerning from below. Listening with a third ear, waiting for the Real to disclose itself, and receiving that disclosure are the first three steps in the process of discernment from below. The person who does not pray cannot discern at all; the prayerful person is the discerning person.

2. *Consciousness-examen.* This renewal of the old particular examen looks at life in a reflective way, trying to distinguish patterns that are salutary from

patterns that are destructive. I look at my life as it reverberates in the center of my existence, not "as on a screen in front of me," as Thomas Clarke says, but from the inside out, taking the feelings of the day to my center, and "in that quiet feel their pulse, so to speak, or taste their flavor."[21] In this way I come to recognize my patterns for good or ill, to identify where God is acting in my life, where I am being fooled by the demonic.

3. *Review of Life.* A kindred group analyzes together a fact of one person's experience in the piercing light of faith. Insights are shared, a gospel judgment rendered, and a decision taken pro or con the Christian reality of that experience. This is a method of translating the gospel into particular environments of the 20th century.

4. *Journal.* The journal uses the catalyst of writing to concretize and symbolize one's own experience. It is my story, not in diary form or in rational analysis or introspection, but flowing onto the page from my heart and feelings, and thus in images and symbols as well as rational discourse. The journal is my feelings, moods, and aspirations expressed in imagery strictly for my own eyes. It is a companion along the way. The unconscious breaks into awareness through being translated in this way. The thoughts and reflections break out onto the page and our unconscious depths guide the pen. Thus the journal reveals our selves to ourselves.

5. *Counseling.* Counseling deals primarily with our emotions, whereas guidance is informational in intent, and spiritual direction attempts to evaluate, hence discern religious experiences. Spiritual direction moves closer to counseling in proportion to the discernment proceeding less from above and more

from below. Counseling presupposes a certain skill in dealing with the dynamics of the psyche and communicating these insights; it becomes spiritual counseling, when the intent is the sharing of the secrets of the heart, which are the object of spiritual discernment.

6. *Healing.* Inner healing or the healing of memories is the process of recalling past hurts, real or suspected, recognized or still buried in the unconscious, and allowing these to surface in the loving atmosphere of prayer that evokes the presence of God. The healing comes from the conscious acceptance of the hurt or its scars, and this is made possible through the loving presence of one who accepts you unconditionally, namely, the Lord who is mediated to you through the praying community or the minister.

7. *Dreams.* Dreams are nature's way of expressing freely what is going on in the unconscious and blocked in some way from emerging into consciousness. To cultivate an awareness of what is happening in the dream and to be friendly to this material even without understanding its precise significance is a therapeutic experience. It is also revelatory. Dreams become more helpful if some professional person can help interpret the meaning of the dreams.

SIX

CONCLUSION

Discernment neither seeks nor desires to put God
in a box or trivialize the mystery of his incompre-
hensibility and infinite love. Thus the process and all
proposed methods are part of an ongoing search, the
kind of search that marked the Blessed Virgin Mary's
whole life. Mary pondered God's word, keeping all
that happened and all that was said in the depths of
her heart. She strove to understand, but was sure only
of her faith and trust. These attitudes were the light in
the darkness that "guided her more surely than the
dawn."[22] The particulars always remain in the
shadow, and discernment is an ongoing quest. Mary
illustrates Pascal's words from Jesus: "You would not
be seeking me unless you had already found me."

I would close with a quotation from an excellent
analysis of the effect of Freud and Marx on contemporary spiritual discernment. The author seizes
the limitations and possibilities of authentic discernment. He writes:

This concept of the Christian process of discernment
. . . as a process in which this truth and will of God
becomes known in the course of their coming about

supposes a critically overt admission that we possess no *external* criterion guaranteeing our faithfulness to God. It supposes explicit and conscious acceptance of the *theoretical obscurity* of our faith and the practical *opacity* of our sinful life . . .

Psychoanalysis and Marxist analysis can help us to see that *Christian hope* is the opposite extreme of the sin of trying to *idealize* God in order to manipulate Him at our will and thereby feel *secure*. Psychoanalysis and Marxist analysis can, in a word help us to understand that the discernment of truth is, for the Christian, nothing other than the *truth of his discernment* in the same way that the meeting "with God" in this life is nothing other than our tireless search "for Him."[23]

We discern as long as we are searching; the process stops when we cease to search.

EPILOGUE

From the foregoing discernment may come off as impossibly complicated. In fact, it is both complicated and it is simple, because it is "the examined life."

The questions it asks are beyond definitive answers: who am I? What makes me tick? Where am I going? What am I doing with my life, my work, my relationships? These are general questions that allow general responses. They also can be answered on many levels. Discernment asks them about concrete, individual moments, decisions, events and experiences. It has in view, moreover, ultimate aspects, since it searches for the presence and absence of God. By definition God is "the Beyond in the midst of life." The closer we get to him, the more he recedes into inaccessible light.

The task of discernment is thus a formidable one, and in view of the changing and developing stages of life it is inevitably complicated. But it is also simple, since it strives basically for awareness. It seeks to become more aware of what God is doing in our lives. This is achieved by our awareness of changing moods and the meanings these represent, by our getting in touch with the patterns that are our truth and that resonate with our whole being, by our consciousness of what helps and what hinders our wholeness and growth. Discernment offers only a general sense of God working in our lives. It does not tell us what to do, since it moves on a different plane from the technical. But it does indicate whether or not we are moving in the right direction on the deepest level of our being, and in this way it enlightens our experiences, reinforces our decisions, and concretizes our desire to find God in all things.

Expectations from discernment vary according to the personality and religious culture of individuals. Some persons hope to find specific and detailed directives from God in their discernment. They seek to identify, not just the authenticity of the process of their life, but the products of this activity.[24] This means that they try to discern the objective questions of their existence, from their vocation in life such as marriage or religious life to the precise ministry or exact location of their present commitment. Obviously there is a vast spectrum of possibilities here, from the general conditions through the particular to the individual choices. The common denominator is "product:" the choice is seen to be the God-inspired result of the process of discernment.

My own bias favors a less fulsome expectation. Discernment does not penetrate the mystery of God's workings and always leaves us in the obscurity of faith. It tells us only that the process is authentic and that we are, therefore, acting "in the Lord." It tells us that the Lord is near, indeed within, but we remain searchers of his holy will. We are guaranteed only that our hearts are right and our subjective activity is in God's truth and love. Conceivably we may well come to conclusions and decisions that are ill-taken from other points of view than the spiritual. Thus the divine guidance of discernment does not give, at least ordinarily, any absolute or infallible answers. It merely helps us "keep our eyes fixed on Jesus" (Heb. 12:2) in the conflictual situations of life.

But in everyone's view discernment does bespeak the Silent Presence of God. Its whole point is to put or keep us in touch with God in the concreteness of life-in-the-world. Other ways of practicing discernment might be fashioned, but the process we have emphasized is a psychological one. It is based on plumbing our feelings and the reasons for them, on reflecting on our subjectivity and interiority, on examining our actions and following their strands to their roots in our Christ-self or our shadow. In this process images that rise spontaneously from the well of our unconscious are particularly revelatory. Whether they are pictures or music or movement like the dance, they catch and express ourselves to ourselves. Such images, or better, symbols pull together our fragmented consciousness and our mysterious unconscious.

Our faith conviction is that these psychic expressions — feelings, images, thoughts, self-understandings, behavior — reveal our inner, spiritual truth and, therefore, the Silent Presence within. How effective is this approach? The method depends greatly on our psychological and spiritual maturity. If we are ambivalent and divided by chaotic emotions and neurotic conditions, our affective states will provide no positive guidance. Our task will be to understand our condition and bring order and discipline into our affective life. But as we come to achieve that discipline, in proportion as "we die and our lives are hidden with Christ in God" (Col. 3:3), the methodology we have proposed becomes more effective. Commensurate with our spiritual freedom and surrender to God, to be in touch with ourselves is to be in touch with the word of God that is ourselves.

In the final analysis discernment is gift in the same sense and by the same growth process as prayer and contemplation. Just as prayer is contact with God or sheer illusion, as C.S. Lewis was fond of saying, so discernment is awareness of the in-breaking of God into our lives or mere introspection. The journey into self, moving within the perspectives of the world of faith, actuates that faith and puts us in touch with the Silent Presence. Such is the rich contribution of discernment to life in the Spirit.

FOOTNOTES

1. In *The Dynamic Element in the Church, Quaestiones disputatae* 12, New York, 1964, 84-156, at. 115.

2. The collection of essays edited by C. Floristán and Christian Duquoe and published as a volume of *Concilium* n. 119, under the title *Discernment of the Spirit and of Spirits* (New York, 1979) is one of the better recent studies on the topic. It rightly distinguishes the project of locating the Spirit from the interpretation of the affective impulses, sentiments, feelings and emotions called "spirits." The former is the goal, the latter a means. See also the useful distinctions drawn by John C. Futrell, S.J., "Ignatian Discernment," in *Studies in the Spirituality of Jesuits,* 2 (April, 1970), 47-48.

3. Fernando Urbina, "Movements of Religious Awakening and Christian Discernment of Spirits," in *Concilium* n. 89, *Spiritual Revivals,* New York, 1971, 64.

4. In the introduction to *Discernment of Spirits,* a collection of articles from The Dictionnaire de Spiritualité, Collegeville, 1970, 9.

5. 39 (March, 1980), 198.

6. *The Divine Milieu,* New York, 1960, 95-101.

7. In *America,* March 15, 1980.

8. St. John of the Cross, *The Living Flame of Love,*
   I, 7, in *The Collected Works of St. John of the
   Cross,* tr. K. Kavanaugh, O.C.D., and O. Rod-
   riguez, O.C.D., Washington, D.C., 1973, 582.

9. *Summa contra Gentiles,* III, 154.

10. John C. Futrell, S.J., "Ignatian Discernment,"
    Studies in the Spirituality of Jesuits, 2 (1970),
    50-52.

11. *The Ascent of Mount Carmel,* II, 26, 11, in *The
    Collected Works,* 196. This important chapter
    connects the mainline mystical experience of con-
    templation with the word of prophecy. Unlike the
    contemplation, which is the general, loving, in-
    communicable knowledge of God derived from
    mystical union, "for it is itself that very union,"
    (n. 5) the word of prophecy regards "the truths of
    things in themselves and the deeds and events of
    men." (n. 11) Sometimes this knowledge is
    miraculous, but other times it is a connatural side-
    effect of the highly endowed state of infused
    contemplation. See n. 13. The word of prophecy
    in this case belongs to the area of discernment.

12. See Bernard J. F. Lonergan, S.J., *Method in
    Theology,* New York, 1972, 105-107.

13. This quotation is taken from a privately prepared
    unpublished instruction based upon George A.
    Aschenbrenner's deservedly famous article, "Con-
    sciousness Examen," in *Review for Religious* 31
    (1972), 14-21 and still available as a reprint.

14. Thomas Dubay, S.M., *Authenticity,* Denville,
    New Jersey, 1977, 10-11.

15. In *Lonergan Workshop,* Volume I, ed. Fred Lawrence, Missoula, Mont., 1978, 187-222.

16. *The Living Flame of Love,* I, 21, in *Collected Works,* 587.

17. Argus Communications paperback, Niles, Illinois, 1974, 333. Cited by Moore, loc. cit., 209.

18. In *America,* April 24, 1976, 357-358.

19. *The Interior Castle,* VII:2, n. 7, in *Collected Works of St. Teresa of Avila,* II, tr. K. Kavanaugh, O.C.D. and O. Rodriguez, O.C.D., Washington, DC, 1980, 435-436.

20. *The Making of a Mind,* New York, 1965, p. 251.

21. "Finding Grace at the Center," in *The Way;* 7 (1977), 21.

22. "The Dark Night," 4th stanza, in *Collected Works,* 296.

23. Enrique M. Urena, "Christian Discernment, Psychoanalysis, and Marxist Analysis," in *Concilium* n. 119, *Discernment of the Spirit and of Spirits,* New York, 1979, 71.

24. This useful distinction is developed by Frances Dorff, O. Praem., "The Heart of Progoff's Process Spirituality," *Review for Religious,* 29 (1980) 389-403.